AF073917

Also by Amy and Lee Draper

The Magical Rainbow Babies

 *in*

The Brightest Star in the Sky

Amy and Lee Draper
Illustrated by Sean Webster

Text copyright © Amy and Lee Draper 2021
magical_rainbow_babies@hotmail.com
Illustrations copyright © Sean Webster 2021

Published by Elephant Memoirs
www.elephant-memoirs.co.uk
Printed by Book Printing UK

Amy and Lee Draper have asserted their right under the Copyright, Designs and Patents Act 1988 to be identified as the authors of this work.

British Library Cataloguing in Publication Data
A catalogue record for this book is available from the British Library.
ISBN 978-1-8383332-2-5

All rights reserved. No part of this publication may be reproduced, stored in a retrieval system, or transmitted, in any form or by any means without the prior written permission of the publisher, nor be otherwise circulated in any form or binding or cover other than that in which it is published and without a similar condition being imposed on the subsequent purchaser.

Although every precaution has been taken in the preparation of this book, the publisher and author assume no responsibility for errors or omissions. Neither is any liability assumed for damages resulting from the use of information contained herein.

Printed on FSC accredited paper.

For Charlie, the brightest star in our sky,

and our three rainbow babies, Dolly, Winnie and Reenie.

Dolly and Winnie are in the park
On a beautiful and hot sunny day.
They have just finished playing on the swings,
And their friend Lucy is coming their way.

Lucy has a big smile.
Lucy has some news!
The girls are so excited,
They can't stay in their shoes!

Lucy has a brand-new baby brother!

He's in the big blue pram.

He's got curly hair and brown eyes,

And his name is Sam.

The girls are so so happy!
This is the best news ever.
All the friends together,
Enjoy the lovely weather.

They play on the roundabout, see-saw and slide,
Round and round, up and down.
They play until they get so tired
They need to lie on the ground.

With nothing but laughter,
Lying on the grass,
Lucy says, "There's a question
That I just have to ask!"

"I know you've got each other,
But wouldn't you both like
To have a baby brother?"

Dolly and Winnie reply,
"But we DO have a baby bro.
Didn't you two know?"

Lucy looks confused...
"I've never seen you out playing
With your brother," she says, bemused.

Winnie says,
"We can't take him to the park,
Or play with him on the swings.

But that will never stop
The love that he still brings."

Dolly says,
"We can't stand and watch him,
 Going down the slide.

But being Charlie's sisters,
Fills us both with pride."

Lucy says, "How?"

"You see, Lucy," say the girls,
"Although he isn't with us now,
We love him though we are apart,
And he is forever in our hearts."

"We just close our eyes,
And see him in our minds.
And we've got to tell you,
He really is one of a kind."

In a flitter and a flurry
And a swish and swoosh,
All of a sudden, the clouds start to glow.

It's Charlie, in the magical rainbow!

Later that day, the girls ask Charlie,
"Where have you been all day?"

Charlie says, "Never worry.
I'm up here, watching you play.

If you ever miss me,
That is quite alright.
You can always find me,
As I am here at night."

"Look at all the brightest lights,
And find the brightest star.

I will always shine on you,
And be wherever you are!"

ACKNOWLEDGEMENTS

To all the staff at Liverpool Women's Hospital and Alder Hey Hospital

A special thanks to:
Sue Draper, Keith Draper, Emma Grice, Alan Grice, Rita Knight, Ella McPhillips, Graham Knight, Charlie McPhillips, Elsie and Jack Draper, Nanny McMahon, Frank and Val McMahon, Betty Law, Joe McPhillips, Catherine Elliott, Catherine Perry, Joseph Pomford

All our parents, grandparents, aunties, uncles, cousins and friends,
for supporting our on-going journey

Find us at
@magical_rainbow_babies
@thedrapergirls

About the Authors

We are a husband and wife duo, Amy and Lee Draper. Our stories are loosely based on personal accounts from our own family. We lost our first child in November 2010, but we talk about Charlie all the time. We now have three rainbow girls, and we need to explain to them where their brother has gone. We wanted a story about Charlie that our children could relate to. As we couldn't find one on the market at the time, we decided to write a series of books ourselves.

I, Amy, am a neonatal nurse, and have been since 2015. I work in neonatal units all over the north-west of England. I have seen many rainbow babies, and understand the challenges parents go through. Hopefully, these books will support parents and carers in the future.

The aim of our books is to help all parents of rainbow babies, but most of all to remember the little angels who have gained their wings.

Charities to support parents and siblings

Child Death Helpline – Freephone 0800 282 986.

Love, Jasmine - www.lovejasmine.org.uk

Sands - www.sands.org.uk

The Lullaby Trust - www.lullabytrust.org.uk

Sibling Support - www.siblingsupport.co.uk

Winston's Wish – www.winstonswish.org

Darcey's Dream - www.darceysdream.com/sibling-support

*Just put one foot in front of the other,
and deal with today.
Every day after will follow.*

Be kind to yourself.